Anger
Natural Treatments to Manage Frustration and Stress

By James Seals

2nd Edition

Table of Contents

Introduction

Everyone experiences anger at some time in their lives, although did you know the damage that anger can do to those who go too far. You know that you have stepped over the boundary when anger causes you stress and tension. This impacts how you feel inside and makes the situation worse, rather than better. If you find yourself angry or frustrated, then it's time to learn natural ways to curb that anger and to make your life a better place to be.

This book covers a lot of territory showing you the way forward. It's a lesson worth learning if you know that your anger is getting the best of you because that little monster inside you may be responsible for making your life unhappy. People around you may also be adversely affected and it's time to learn how to control anger and become a better and healthier person.

How do you express anger? When is too much anger harming you? You need to get back in control and this book discusses natural ways that you can find your way forward out of anger into a place of peaceful response. When you do, you will improve relationships and your own peace of mind, as well as improving your health. Read on, and improve your life.

Chapter 1: What is Anger?

Anger is a natural emotion, and it is one that we all experience at some time or other in our lives. It can range in intensity from being mildly irritated to erupting like a volcano in full pyroclastic flow and is the way in which we react to something we perceive as a danger. There are three different components to anger:

- A physical reaction that starts with an adrenaline rush. Your heart rate and blood pressure increase and your muscles tighten up. This is your body's fight or flight response
- A cognitive reaction that comes from how you perceive what has caused the anger, i.e. did something happen or was something said that you perceive to have been unfair?
- The behavioral reaction, which is the way your anger is expressed. This covers a wide range of reactions from looking and sounding angry to physical reactions, such as shouting and slamming doors, or any other way in which you demonstrate your displeasure at the situation.

Anger is natural; it is how you manage that is what counts and mismanaged anger is what causes problems, is highly unproductive and is not healthy, either for you or for those around you. Normal anger helps you to see clearly about things, solve problems and make decisions that work to your advantage.

The causes of anger are many and varied. Anger management is something that you are taught, whether consciously or not. We learn from those around us, our families, friends and the culture we live in. You may have been brought up in an environment where mismanaged anger was the norm, in which case, you are more likely to respond in a negative manner to feelings of anger.

Chapter 2: How We Express Anger

It is instinct to react to anger with aggression; it is an adaptive response to what we perceive as a threat and anger can inspire some very powerful behaviors in people. These behaviors allow us to defend against the threat and, therefore, anger is an important emotion for our survival, to a certain extent.

That said, it would not be right, or fair, to attack every person or object that creates those feelings of anger and, on occasion, common sense must come into play. For most people, the response to anger is both conscious and unconscious and there are three approaches to dealing with anger:

- Expressing your feelings in a manner that is not aggressive is healthy. You must learn the difference between assertive and aggressive and make sure you use the right response.
- Suppressing the anger is when you turn your energies and thoughts to something else, usually something more positive and more constructive. However, anger needs to be expressed and holding in it can turn it on you and cause health problems, such as expression, and hypertension, which can also lead to an increased risk of a heart attack

- Calming is when you control how you react internally. You take the necessary steps needed to bring your heart rate and blood pressure back down to safe levels and allow the feelings to die down.

When we talk about anger management, we are talking about how you control your emotional and physiological responses to situations that cause anger. You cannot avoid these situations and you cannot avoid becoming angry at times; that is only natural. However, you can learn to control how you react.

As you already know, anger comes in many different forms and different types affect different people in different ways. Not all signs of anger are verbal or even obvious to start with although you can tell when someone is angry, just by their body language and tone of voice. Some people use body language more than words, perhaps trying to make themselves look bigger and more intimidating, clenching their teeth and hands, staring and frowning. Others are very good at keeping their anger inside, making it very difficult to see that they are angry; it is rare for this type of person to attack physically without some kind of warning signs first.

Anger is used, at a basic level, as a form of protection, a response to a perceived threat against you, your loved ones or your territory. There are other reasons for anger, some of them rational and some of them irrational. If your anger is irrational, it could be that you struggle to manage or can't even accept that you are angry. Some of the more common triggers of anger include:

- Grief
- Sadness
- Rudeness
- Poor interpersonal skills
- Tiredness
- Hunger
- Injustice, i.e. infidelity, bullying, humiliation, etc.

- Sexual frustration
- Feeling of disappointment or failure
- Alcohol and/or drugs – either after taking them or during a period of withdrawal
- Stress
- Debt or money-related problems
- A criminal offence against you or a loved one, i.e. theft, burglary, sexual offence
- Inappropriate treatment
- Illness – physical or mental
- Pain

Chapter 3: How Much Is Too Much Anger?

There are tests that can measure feelings of anger and their intensity. These tests can tell you how well you handle anger and whether you are prone to feeling it more or less. However, there is a pretty good chance that, if you already suffer with anger management problems, you already know about it. If you do have a problem with managing anger and you can recognize it, that's the first step. The next is to get help.

Some people are far more prone to outbursts than others are; they react more easily and more extremely to situations than other people and the feelings they experience are far more intense.

On the opposite side of the coin, there are those who barely acknowledge a situation that should make them angry. And, in the middle, are those who don't explode with anger, instead they show their irritation by being grumpy and irritable, sometimes with the wrong people.

So, how much is too much anger? That is a difficult question to answer because every person is different. However, if you are or know someone who is angry all the time, who explodes at the slightest provocation, then there is a good chance that he or she, or you, are holding too much anger.

Some people have a low tolerance level for frustrating situations. They cannot take things calmly, especially if they feel they have been unjustly or unfairly treated, even if it is only minor. What makes people this way is a mystery. For some people it is genetic, for others, it may be a sociocultural problem.

We are taught from an early age that anger is bad, it is a negative response and, in some cases, it can be. But, being taught this stops us from knowing how to handle it properly. The main lesson is to pinpoint what it is that triggers your feelings of anger and develop methods to deal with those triggers and that is where anger management comes into play.

Different Types of Anger

Anyone who says that they have never been angry, throughout their whole life is either lying or does not recognize anger. Anger is an emotion that everyone experiences at some time or another, some people more so than others. However, not all anger is the same; there are a number of different types and differing degrees of anger and angry emotions. Anger can be highly destructive and can result in a lot of different problems; while anger in itself is a healthy emotion, how you channel it is important. Knowing which type of anger you are dealing with is a good start in knowing how to handle it and how to channel it correctly.

Behavioral Anger

This is often displayed through aggressive and physical actions, either against a person or against something else that is responsible or perceived as being responsible for triggering the emotion. This type of anger almost always results in a physical attack on the subject, either physical abuse or assault.

Passive Anger

People who display passive anger tend to use nonphysical weapons, such as cynicism ad sarcasm. They may also be very quiet but this only so that they avoid any type of confrontation. They are very good at keeping their feelings hidden but are often to be found sulking about something and this is how their anger will manifest itself.

Verbal Anger

This type of anger is, as the name implies, expressed using words and not physical actions. People who exhibit this type of anger will use criticism, insults or verbal abuse and will be judgmental as a way of putting people down and showing their anger.

Self-inflicted Anger

Self-inflicted anger is a way for people to show their anger by taking it out on themselves. People who use self-inflicted anger to punish themselves for something they perceive they have done or that someone else has done to them. They will use a number of different methods, from starving themselves, to inflicting actual injuries on their own bodies.

Volatile Anger

This kind of anger is often compared to a volcano because of the speed at which it can erupt. One moment a person will be calm and the next, in a towering rage. There is often no warning, it will explode out of nowhere and it may even go unnoticed. Volatile anger is generally the result of pent up emotions, which could otherwise have been expressed in a healthier way.

Chronic Anger

Chronic anger is prolonged and there is usually no reason for it.

People who suffer from chronic anger get so used to getting angry that it just becomes a habit and they will often get angry at something that would not affect any other person.

Judgmental Anger

Those who exhibit judgmental anger will criticize others, put them down and make them feel very unsure about themselves. They will make other people feel worthless and unsure about their abilities. Judgmental anger is strongly related to verbal anger and both may be displayed at the same time.

Overwhelmed Anger

Overwhelmed anger is usually exhibited by fighting and shouting, as a way of relieving stress. People who have this usually find that they cannot cope with what is happening around them and they tend to bottle things up until they cannot take anymore.

Retaliatory Anger

Retaliatory anger is exhibited as a direct reaction to another person lashing out. It is a very common type of anger, the one seen most often and can be highly damaging as the person rarely thinks before they lash out.

Paranoid Anger

Feelings of insecurity and jealousy are what tend to trigger off this kind of anger. T may manifest itself when a person feels that they have been missed out, or something that they feel is theirs has been given to someone else. They may also feel intimidated by others and will lash out.

Deliberate Anger

Deliberate anger is manifested when a person wants control over a situation or person or by someone who is frustrated. It will often happen when things don't turn out the way that was expected or when things don't go according to plan.

Now let's have a look at some of these forms of anger in more detail.

Chronic Anger

Prolonged chronic anger can be damaging to the health as it will affect the immune system and can also cause mental disorders. It is problematic because, more often than not, the anger that manifests itself is way out of proportion to the cause – if there even is a cause. This can lead to stress, which leads to other health conditions as well as having the potential to be self-destructive. The person may also exhibit violence towards others.

Conditions and Symptoms

If you suffer with anger, answer the following questions honestly to see if the conditions are consistent and chronic manner:

1. Is your anger out of proportion to the cause? Do not include the normal snappiness that we all tend to exhibit when stressed or in a bad mood. Think about angry outbursts that happen over something that is quite trivial and wouldn't cause most people to react.
2. Do you feel intense anger when you think about things that have happened in the past or people who are significant in your life for one reason or another? This might be quite vague but think about anything that could have happened in the past or the people who are were or are in your life. It could be something that is quite insignificant to other people but causes you to exhibit extreme and intense anger.
3. Do you find yourself angry for no reason? There is no apparent cause, just experiencing anger at nothing.

4. Do you find that people are guarded when they interact with you? Think about the way you interact with others and think about whether people tend to be cautious around you, trying hard not to upset you.

5. Are there people in your life that have stopped contacting you or talking to you and try to avoid being around you? You could start to feel intense loneliness as your anger drives people away and you end up convincing yourself that it is you who doesn't want to contact them. This may be true in certain cases, especially if the other person is one that causes you to feel anger.

6. Have you harmed yourself because of your anger? Not just physical injury but possibly making bad business deals, getting into trouble because you have been snappy with a customer, picking up a traffic violation or damaging property.

7. Has anyone ever told you that you may have a problem with anger? Has more than one person told you this on a number of occasions? This is your wake up call. While an isolated incident may be just that, if several people say the same thing, you should seriously listen to them and seek the appropriate help.

Passive Anger

Passive anger tends to be hidden and will be exhibited in ways that are not always obvious. In some cases, you may not even be aware that you are showing signs of repressed anger and this is what it makes it one of the single most difficult forms to diagnose or identify. Passive anger is generally expressed through sarcastic comments, avoiding others or by subpar performance, arriving late, leaving early. An example of this is an employee who is not satisfied; they may begin to get back at their employer by working below their abilities, less productively and will often not even be aware they are doing it unit they are pulled up on it. Other examples include:

- **Lack of communication** – especially when there is a clear problem that needs talking about
- **Avoidance** – because you are too angry to speak calmly and rationally
- **Evading** – burying your head in the sand because you don't want to deal with an issue
- **Procrastination** – putting off important tasks deliberately in favor of those that are not important
- **Obstruction** – Deliberately preventing an event or stalling change
- **Fear of Competition** – Avoiding a situation where one person will be seen as being better at something than you are
- **Ambiguous** – Not engaging fully in a conversation and when you do being vague, cryptic or unclear
- **Sulking** – Staying quiet, sullen, morose and resentful to gain the attention or sympathy of others
- **Chronic lateness** – Putting yourself in control of others
- **Chronic Forgetfulness** - Showing a blatant disregard of others as a form of punishment
- **Making Excuses** - Always coming up with one reason or another as a way of getting out of doing things
- **Victimization** – Not able to see your own part in a situation and turning the tables to make you out to be the victim and behaving as the victim as well
- **Self-pity** – The poor me routine to gain sympathy
- **Blaming** – instead of taking responsibility, you blame others for a situation because you are unable to or do not want to see the situation as a whole
- **Withholding** – Stopping normal behaviors like cooking, sex, making drinks, etc. to reinforce a message to other people – a message that is already completely unclear anyway
- **Learned Helplessness** – Continually acting as if you ae unable to help yourself and deliberately making a bad job of something for which you are solely responsible

Passive anger is often seen as a defense mechanism, a form of protection. It may be as a result of something that happened early on in life or it may just be an automatic response but whatever the person is protecting themselves from will be unique to that person and will more than likely include feelings of fear, rejection, loneliness, mistrust, insecurity or low self-esteem.

Overwhelmed Anger

This is generally caused by too many demands, making a person struggle to cope. The following are ten signs that a person is overwhelmed and may end up causing trouble if they don't or can't calm down. When a person is overwhelmed or flooded, their blood pressure and heart rate are high and the prefrontal cortex function in the brain is dropping. This is the part of the brain that controls what you say and do and, when it drops, it causes you to say and do things you wish you hadn't. You cannot have a proper conversation with a person who is at this stage and the following signs are designed to tell you what the other person is feeling, to let you know when they are overwhelmed and heading for an angry confrontation:

1. If the person you are talking to shuts their eyes, they are telling you that they cannot deal with too much more, they have heard enough. Do not mistake this for a blink. Most of us do it, shut our eyes for a second or more when we can't take in any more information or deal with what is being said

2. If the person you are talking to looks away, maybe closing their eyes as well, this is a sign that they are overwhelmed, perhaps angry. Some people do this when they are thinking but be aware that the situation may change at any time.

3. If the person you are talking to turns all or part of their body away, they are either running or regrouping to attack. Back off from the person that does this and give them some space

4. If their voice starts to get louder it's a good sign that the anger is close to the surface
5. If the pitch of the voice gets higher, they are stressed and are on the defensive. This is a clear sign for you to back off.
6. If the pitch of the voice drops, take notice! This could be the sign of an attack and you are in the direct line of fire
7. Watch the facial expressions, as these are one of the biggest giveaways. A person who is scowling, has wide eyes, or squints may be telling you that they are overwhelmed. Do not ignore it and most definitely do not push them
8. If the person rolls their eyes, they could be showing contempt or you are not taking you seriously because they are already overwhelmed.
9. Listen for verbal cues, like sighing and grunting.
10. If you notice that the person's hands are tense, fists are clenched or the hands are shaking, back off immediately.

Pay close attention to all of these cues because they are warning signs that you are pushing too hard and the end result will not be pretty. Meltdowns often manifest themselves in angry tears, shouting and sometimes violence and none of that is productive behavior. If you are the person who is overwhelmed, never say to the person you are communicating with, or your partner, that you need a timeout. Tell them why you need a timeout, that the relationship is too important and you may do or say something that will damage it. Make it clear that you are not just stomping off in a huff, that you have real concerns.

Self-Inflicted Anger

This is a way of punishing yourself without taking your anger out on another person. The reasons are usually that the person perceives as something they have done or that someone else has done to them that cause anger and the normal result is self-injury. Self-injury is a psychiatric disorder that is fully recognized and is not seen as a suicide attempt. Although the person does not have the intent to kill themselves, there are some forms of self-injury that can lead to serious medical care being required and, in some cases, can lead to death. People who practice self-injury often try to hide it from others and it can be difficult to spot the symptoms at first. Some of those symptoms include:

- Scarring, perhaps from burns or from cuts
- Fresh scratches or cuts
- Bruises
- Bald spots or hair loss
- Broken bones
- Always having sharp objects to hand
- Spending a lot of time alone
- Wearing clothes that cover the legs and arms, even in hot conditions
- Claiming that they are clumsy, frequently having accidents

Self-injury is very different from other forms of "mutilation" that are socially acceptable, such as tattoos or piercings. Self-injury is an unhealthy result of the struggle to cope with too much emotion, such as shame, sadness, rage, fear terror or intense anger.

The Effects of Self-Injury

Self-injury is often a highly impulsive act and is usually planned, seen as something of a ritual and the injury is inflicted in a very methodical and controlled manner. It is repetitive – it is rare that you will find a self-harmer who does it just the once. The most common places are the arms, legs and torso because they are the easiest to reach and the easiest to hide from view. Cutting is the most common form, using a sharp instrument to scratch or cut the body, but there are other forms as well, including:

- Cutting
- Burning
- Poisoning
- Taking an overdose

- Carving symbols or complete words on the skin
- Breaking a bone
- Hitting or punching, leaving bruises
- Head banging
- Biting
- Pulling hair out
- Not allowing wounds to heal

The Causes of Self-Injury

While self-injury may bring about a sense of peace, this does not last long and is usually followed by feelings of intense guilt, shame and a return of the emotions that caused it in the first place. Some people who self-injure suffer from any one of a number of mental illnesses, including:

- Depression
- Anorexia/Bulimia
- Post-traumatic stress disorders
- Borderline personality disorder

It is a complex mix of emotions that can causes a person to self-injure but it is normally as a result of being unable to cope with pain and anger in a healthy way. It can affect anybody, from young teens to older adults, male or female. There are certain factors that may increase the risk, including:

- **Age** – Most female self-harmers are adolescents. Self-injury generally starts in early teens at a time when the emotions are forever changing and highly volatile. Young females generally fear being alone and find themselves in conflict with both authority and parental figures.
- **Family History** - there is evidence to suggest that self-injury is common in those who have a family history of suicide, self-destruction and self-injury

- **Life Issues** - This is more in the case of female self-harmers who have been emotionally, physically or sexually abused. They may also have been neglected as children or are socially isolated. Unemployment and divorce can also play a large part.
- **Mental Health Problems** – Self-injury is commonly associated with some mental conditions, including substance abuse, eating disorder, PTSD, BPD, depression and anxiety disorders.
- **Substance abuse** - Many people who self-harm do so when they are under the influence of drugs or alcohol or during a withdrawal period.

Chapter 4: What Harm Is Anger Doing To You?

A certain amount of anger is good for you but too much can actually be causing you physical and emotional harm. If you are frequently angry, the flow of stress chemicals, alongside the metabolic changes that accompany them, can cause an awful lot of different conditions:

- Headaches
- Problems with digestion
- Pains in the abdomen
- Inability to sleep properly
- An increase in anxiety levels
- Depression
- Hypertension
- Eczema and other skin conditions
- Stroke
- Heart attack

While learning to cope with your anger can help many of these conditions to disappear, the long-term damage may already be done in some cases and it can take you much longer to heal. Looking at the last condition, how many people actually realize that frequent bouts of anger can exponentially raise their risks of a heart attack?

There has been a lot of research carried out on the link between stress and anger and the effects it has on the heart and cardiovascular system. While moderate anger may not be too much of an issue, provided it is not on a constant basis, high levels of anger can contribute to heart disease.

How? Much of it comes down to the "fight or flight" response your body displays when you show anger or hostility. These are direct psychological effects – when stress hormones, such as cortisol and adrenaline, are released, your heart rate gets faster, along with your breathing rate. A direct result of that is high blood pressure, which, as we are all aware, is a precursor for heart disease.

While this is a natural response that could get you out of trouble on occasion, if it happens constantly, it will cause a great deal of wear and tear on your cardiovascular system and the heart. Frequent angry outbursts have been related to a speeding up of atherosclerosis, a disease in which there is a buildup on the arteries of fatty plaque. This causes the heart to work harder and pump faster, while the plaque is constricting the vessels, causing your blood pressure to shoot up.

High levels of blood sugar or glucose appear in the blood and this results in more globules of fat in the blood vessels, leading, eventually, to the walls of the arteries suffering damage.

Chapter 5: What Is Anger Management and How Can It Help You?

Anger management is a process or series of processes that help you to learn how to recognize when you are becoming angry. It helps you to learn how to take action to calm yourself down and work out how to deal with the situation that has caused your anger in a positive rather than negative manner.

The one thing anger management does not do is stop you from feeling anger nor does it tell you that you must hold it in. Anger is natural and needs to be let out while holding it in can cause a lot more harm in the long run, both physically and emotionally on you and those around you. In short, anger management is about teaching you how to express your anger.

There are plenty of ways that you can learn to manage your anger. Books, websites, classes, even therapy but, whichever route you choose the end result is that you will learn to recognize your frustrations early enough to resolve them positively, remaining in control and calm while still getting your point across. Some of the signs that you may need help in managing your anger include:

- Regularly feeling that you have to hold on to your anger and not let it out
- Constantly feeling irritated, cynical, critical, impatient or outright hostility
- Constant arguments with colleagues, family, friends, partner and children
- Physically expressing your anger by lashing out violently
- Making violent threats against property or a person
- Behavior that is frightening and clearly out-of-control, such as reckless driving, breaking things for no reason and hitting out for no apparent reason
- Becoming depressed and anxious about these feelings of anger to the extent that you withdraw

Generally speaking, anger management focuses on learning new skills and a new way of thinking to help you cope with your anger. The aim of any session, including some holistic therapy sessions is to help you to:

- Identify which situations are liable to cause you to become angry and react in a non-aggressive manner BEFORE the anger takes over
- Learn new skills to use when certain situations are liable to trigger feelings of anger
- Recognize when your thinking is not logical and take steps to correct it
- Learn to calm down when things start to affect you
- Learn to express your feelings and your needs in a way that is assertive but not aggressive
- Learn to focus on solving problems logically and calmly
- Learn how to communicate to resolve problems before they get out of control

There are a number of benefits to learning how to control your anger. First, you will feel as though you are actually in control of both a situation and your reaction to it. You will learn how to express yourself in a positive, assertive manner without showing any of the aggression and you will no longer feel that you need to hold in that anger because you will have dealt with it.

Anger management helps you to:

- **Communicate**. It helps you to get your needs across and talk about your frustrations in a way that is positive without allowing your anger to flare up and take over. You will learn how expressing yourself in the right way can help you to stay away from behaviors that may be irrational, impulsive and hurtful, to resolve problems and maintain positivity in any relationship.

- **Stay healthy**. Stress is the biggest cause of many health conditions, such as headaches, backaches, aching joints and muscles, insomnia, problems with digesting food, stomach pains, cardiovascular problems and hypertension, amongst others. This is because of the chemicals released into your body when you show anger and, if you are frequently angry, these chemicals take their toll.

- **Maintain a good level of emotional health.** Anger does not just affect your physical health; it can have a drastic effect on your emotional health, causing depression, anxiety, trouble within your relationships and problems in coping at work and with life in general.

- **Use your frustration positively.** Expressed in the right way, anger can actually be a big motivator in helping you to work harder and take more positive action whereas anger that is inappropriately expressed makes it very difficult for clear thinking and can result in using poor judgment to make decisions.

- **Help you to avoid escape mechanisms that may be addictive.** It is not uncommon for people who suffer from constant and unmanaged anger to turn to smoking, alcohol, food or drugs to help them to cope. Instead of dealing with the problem, this just makes it worse by adding addiction to the list. Anger management helps you to employ techniques that allow you to keep calm and maintain your control without the need to turn to something else.

Chapter 6: The Holistic Approach To Anger Management

While many people turn to their physicians and prescriptions for pills to help them cope with their anger, other, natural, ways help. Holistic therapies are based on the principle that our bodies are interconnected – if one bit goes wrong, it's a sure sign that other bits will suffer too. Holistic therapy works to smooth out any imbalances in our bodies and minds and create positivity in life rather than negativity, which adversely affects the health.

The holistic form of treatment is also based on the premise that the most powerful healer in the world in unconditional love and support and that a person is responsible for their own wellbeing. Other principles of holistic treatment include:

- Everyone has their own built-in powers of healing – you just have to know how to tap into them
- You are a person, you are not a disease and should not be treated as such
- Healing takes a team, not a single player and that team involves you and your doctor. Every part of your life will be addressed with a number of different health practices

- Holistic treatment means fixing what causes the problem, not just taking away what the problem causes.

Holistic doctors use a number of different health practices to treat their patients. Instead of just handing over a prescription for a bottle of pills, the doctor will look at what causes the problem and will draw up a plan to treat every single cause, not just the resulting illness or, in this case, anger management issues. Many holistic doctors turn to lifestyle modifications as a way of treating you, all of which can prove to be far more beneficial in helping you to cope than swallowing medications all day long.

Using Yoga

Yoga is one of the best forms of holistic treatment to help with anger management issues. It teaches you how to be self-aware and in touch with your inner being and, the more in touch with yourself you are, the less likely you are to lash out at the slightest thing.

- Yoga helps in three ways:
- It is a physical form of exercise, an excellent outlet for anger
- You learn techniques for relaxation and deep breathing which will increase you overall sense of peace and calm
- You learn to reach out to your inner self in times of trouble

There are several ways to do yoga, from fast-paced workouts to a slower, more focused method and the best benefits will be reaped when you combine a number of methods together. You should also use yoga in conjunction with the other holistic methods listed below; it certainly isn't a standalone treatment. Below are nine ways to use Yoga to help you to control your anger:

1. **Move Your Body and Use Asanas to Relive Stress**

There are a number of yoga postures that can help you to have a healthy and happy mind and body. Asanas are used to help free tension and negativity pushing it out of the body. Join a class and learn how to do the following asanas:

- Dhanurasana
- Matsyasana
- Janu Shirsasana
- Setubandhasana
- Marjariasana
- Paschimottanasana
- Hastapadasana
- Adhonukha Shwanasana
- Shirshasana
- Shavasana

When you have finished the posture session, lie in Yoga Nidra to allow your mind and body a time to relax completely. This can also help to flush toxins from the body, which are one of the primary causes of stress.

2. **Use Pranayama's to Breathe Properly**

Concentrating on and following the breath can eliminate clutter and negative thoughts from the mind. Learn and try the following:

- Kapal Bhati Pranayama
- Bhastrika Pranayama
- Nadi Shodhan Pranayama
- Bhramari Pranayama

Learn these techniques by either finding the instructions on the Internet or, better yet, joining a class

3. Meditate to Relax your Mind

Meditation is one of the best ways to relax and calm the mind, and it an also teach you how to observe your mind on a daily basis. You will eventually learn to worry only about what is important and let the small stuff get away, reliving your mind of tension, worry and anxiety.

4. Apply the Yoga Philosophy Throughout Your Whole Life

Knowing about ancient Yoga principles and learning to apply it in your daily life can be the secret to a healthy and happy life. For example, the Santosha principle teaches you to understand the value of contentment, while the Aprigraha principle can help you to overcome the desire to possess more and more, or greediness, both of which cause stress and anxiety.

The different niyamas and yamas of Yoga can also help you to eat a balanced diet and change your lifestyle for a healthy one, allowing you to live a more healthy and happy life.

5. Pray, Smile and Keep Faith

Prayer is one of the best forms of support and reassurance that can help to keep you free from anxiety. Developing a habit of praying and chanting daily can help to fill you with positive energy, help to calm the mind and instill a sense of faith that the world and all in it is taken care of by a higher power. Also, make an effort to smile more often, as it will make you feel happier and instill you with a sense of confidence and positivity.

6. Think What you can do for Others, Not for Yourself

When we worry about ourselves all the time, we invite stress into our lives. Instead, turn your attention to what you can do to help

27

others and you will find that you are filled with a sense of joy and satisfaction – all your own worries will melt away.

7. Know That Nothing in the World is Permanent

Once you realize that all around you will change over time, you can relax and settle. You will find yourself freed from anxiety at the realization that, like everything, your problems will pass by and be replaced.

8. Think About a Previous Time Where You Overcame Anxiety

Thinking back to a time when you were able to overcome anxiety and solve a situation will fill you with the courage you need to get past the current issue. Keep thinking about it to give you constant courage

9. Stay in Positive Company

If you spend time with negative people, their negativity rubs off on you. Make sure you only spend time with positive people and you will find that your attitude changes, eventually breeding relaxation, joy and a deep sense of peace.

Chapter 7: Meditation

Meditation is one of the more powerful forms of holistic treatment. When you get angry or stressed out, your adrenal glands secrete cortisol – the angrier you get, the more cortisol is released and this leads to tight muscles, hypertension, racing heart and a surge of adrenaline. Meditation works by rebalancing the cortisol, giving your body a much-needed break and the ability to think more clearly.

Meditation also helps to melt away feelings of stress, anxiety and depression, all of which are causes of anger. It teaches you how to be the master of your emotions and it raises your threshold for stress, making it less likely that you will lose your temper and succumb to the dark energy of anger.

The third benefit of meditation is that it boosts the production of serotonin in your body. Serotonin is known as the "feel good" hormone and, when it is released, it produces feeling of euphoria and happiness, creating a high state of awareness and leaving you feeling much cooler and calmer.

General Guidelines

To get the most out of your meditation sessions, you should follow some general guidelines:

Posture

The way your body is postured affects how the energy flows through and the level of alertness in your mind. The best posture is to sit upright, keeping your spin e straight while still being comfortable. You do not need to get into difficult positions to be able to meditate and, indeed, if you are uncomfortable, you will not relax and you will not gain the full benefits of the meditation. Some meditations need to be done while you are active while, if you are ding meditation that will help you to sleep, you should be lying down.

How Long to Meditate For

A good amount of time is between 15 and 30 minutes although those that are new to it should start with about 5 to 10 minutes and build up. If you meditate on a regular basis, you should try to keep to the same length of time each time.

When to Meditate

This will depend on the type of meditation and the purpose of it. You can meditate at any time of the day but the best times are first thing in the morning or late afternoon. Don't do meditation hat is meant to energize you just before you go to bed – choose one that is designed to help you fall asleep. Deep relaxation meditations are best done before eating or a few hours after a meal.

How Often to Meditate

This will vary for each individual and the reason for meditating. Generally, a couple of times a day is ideal; what is more important is getting into a regular routine. Regular meditation will allow you to reap the benefits much quicker but do be aware that you can overdo it.

Thoughts in Meditation

You cannot stop thoughts from arising into your mind; they are a natural process throughout meditation. Meditation has one goal – to relax you and to make you more at ease with life, at peace with whatever is happening. It is therefore vital that you do not resist whatever comes into your mind during meditation, especially your thoughts.

Never try to resist them or push them to one side. Just notice that they are there and let them take their natural course. When your awareness gets caught up in a train of thought, bring yourself back to focusing on your meditation. This will depend entirely upon the type of meditation you are doing, i.e. in breath meditation bring your focus back to your breath.

You must understand that you are not at fault, have not made a mistake, when thoughts enter your mind or you become absorbed in your thoughts. It is a natural process and, whatever your mind becomes caught up in, you can let go of it. Do not set out to follow the thoughts in your mind, just them go. Allow them to be there but only as a meaningless activity, not as the focus of your meditation.

As your mind starts to settle, you will begin to experience differences in your thinking process. Your thoughts may become vague or you may feel a sense of something that does not get translated into words. Allow this to take place. If you experience a dreamlike state, this is also natural, as is the feeling of having no thoughts at all. All you need to learn is to focus on your meditation and allow things to happen naturally.

Noise

Meditation is more enjoyable if you are in a quiet spot but this isn't always possible. Most meditation can be done in any kind of environment, no matter what the noise level. Do not resist the noise, ignore or block it out. Just let it stay there and focus on your meditation. Everything you hear, see or feel is part of meditation. Just let it happen naturally.

Falling Asleep

You should enter into a state of non-resistance when you are meditating which means that, if you start to fall asleep you should not resist it. If you try to stop yourself from falling asleep, you are straining and that is not the idea of meditation. You are aiming for a state of ease so if sleep comes to you, let it.

Strong Emotions

When you go into state of deep relaxation in meditation, you may sometimes find strong emotions arising. There can be a number of reasons for this. Your mind settles in meditation and it may be that an emotion you have kept hidden or kept at bay by being active and busy, can now surface. It could also be that your mind is unwinding, allowing emotions to be released. A state of meditation is similar to being in a dreamlike state, a time when many issues are being processed.

If there is a specific emotion that makes you uncomfortable, perhaps grief, there may be a tendency to push it out. All emotions, no matter what they are, are life's energy flowing through you and, if you try to stop the flow, the energy gets stuck. If you notice that you are resisting the emotions, stopping them from flowing through stop yourself and let them go. Allow yourself to fully experience the emotion so that the energy can flow through and be resolved.

That said, there could also be a tendency for the mind to get overactive in trying to interpret or dramatize a strong emotion. If, for example, the emotion of anger rises, your mind may find an incident that happened in the past or imagine something that could be happening now, as the cause of that anger. This busyness of the mind works to intensify the emotion and feed it; this stops it from flowing through your body easily. When you feel that you have gotten caught up in a train of thought or some story, let go of it and bring your focus back to the meditation.

If that emotion is too strong for you to bring you focus back easily, you must allow your mind to feel the emotion. Let an awareness of that emotion create a sensation, a physical feeling in the body that you associate with that particular emotion. Let that sensation flow through your body and feel it. If you are fully aware of it, the sensation will eventually dissolve and your mind is free to continue focusing on the meditation.

Finishing the Meditation

You must never end a meditation session too quickly. It is vital that you come out of it slowly because during meditation your mind and body become deeply relaxed and rested. Ending meditation too quickly and suddenly resuming your everyday activities can be a bit of a shock to the system. When your meditation is complete, stay where you are and keep your eyes closed for a couple of minutes. Stretch and move around a little, gradually make yourself a bit more active. When you are ready to resume, open your eyes and slowly begin to "come back to life". Take your time.

Chapter 8: Diet

At some stage in our lives, there is no doubt that we have all been at the stage where we reach for chocolate, alcohol, even a cigarette to calm us down when we feel anger. These are all classed as toxic substances, along with caffeine, and all of them actually have an adverse effect on your mood.

While you may feel the instant gratification as the substance enters your body, you may feel what you perceive to be an instant calming effect, that soon wears off and the withdrawal from the substance, followed by the inevitable cravings for more, will leave you in a more heightened state of anger, much more prone to snappy outbursts.

Looking at your current diet, how much fat and sugary food do you eat? Do you exist on coffee and takeaway foods? Changing your diet can significantly increase your threshold for stress – cutting out sugar, bad fat, and increasing your intake of healthy fruits, vegetables, omega-3 fatty acids and B vitamins will have a real impact on your mood and how you handle stressful situations.

Avoid drinking coffee late at night because your sleep will be disrupted; large meals late at night should be avoided for the same reason. A good night's sleep along with a healthy balanced diet will solve half of the problems you experience in dealing with stress and feelings of anger.

Here we take a closer look at the connection between foods and anger. It is now clear that, through many years of research, certain foods can trigger anger and certain foods can help keep it at bay. According to leading nutritionists and researches, carbs are one of the biggest contributors to feelings of anger. Not all carbs contain what you need to cope with stress, with the day-to-day strain of living. If you eat a lot of these carbs, your body will be deficient in nutrients, vitamins, magnesium and manganese, for example. These deficiencies can make a person more likely to blow a fuse at little things. Research has found that, compared to a group of people who ate healthy fruits, leafy vegetables and beans, those who lived primarily on processed or packaged foods became irritated more easily. In addition, a diet filled with processed foods, causing a deficiency in those important nutrients and vitamins has been linked with violent and aggressive behavior.

On the upside, there are a number of different foods that can help to control feelings of anger and stress. Kiwis, for example, contain a high level of vitamin C, which is a stress-fighting antioxidant. Leafy greens contain the same, along with magnesium, which is a mineral known for helping to relax the muscles and reduce stress and anxiety. Coconut milk is an excellent food source for keeping blood sugar levels regulated and stress levels down. Other foods that do the same are turkey, blueberries, sweet potatoes, dark chocolate and almonds.

Chapter 9: Exercise

Mental and physical health go hand in hand – without one, you cannot satisfactorily have the other. It therefore goes that if you improve your physical health, your ability to manage stress and anger will improve. Anger is normally a result of frustration and anxiety and countless studies have shown that exercise relieves anxiety and depression.

Physical exercise also burns off the excess energy and releases endorphins into the blood that lift your mood, hence the term, "runners high". It reduces blood pressure, which is also a factor in anger, be it the cause or a result. Although all exercise is good for you, some forms are better for anger management than others are:

- **Aerobic Exercise -** produces energy through oxygen and is normally performed for periods of 10 minutes or more at a time. Otherwise known as cardio, aerobic exercise works to raise your heart rate but in a good way by giving the pulmonary system a workout and lowering the blood pressure. Good forms of aerobic exercise are brisk walking, jogging, running, cycling and using a jump rope.

- **Team Exercise** – If you get involved with team sports, you are interacting with others and this has been shown conclusively to reduce stress, provided your interaction with others is positive. The important thing is to avoid contact sports and instead go for roller-skating, basketball or tennis instead.
- **Stationary Exercise** – You do not need to physically get up to exercise. If you suffer from pain or are disabled then chose exercises that you can do seated. One of these is to start at your toes and work your way up your body, tensing and releasing each separate muscle group in turn. This will help you to relax and, combined with deep breathing exercises, to control your temper and reduce your anger.

Chapter 10: Massage Therapy

Massage is generally seen as a way of relaxing and "chilling out" as well as treating specific issues, such as pain, range of movement, etc. The physical benefits of using massage therapy as an anger management technique include:

- Your physical body is more relaxed
- Your circulation improves which in turn, improves cell function, leading to a better feeling of wellbeing
- Tight muscles, pains and aches are relieved
- Releases compression of the nerves
- Increases your mobility and flexibility
- Increases your energy

All of this leads to you feeling much better about yourself and about situations that may cause you to feel anger. Your heart rate will lower, your respiratory rate will ease and your blood pressure will drop back down. As well as that, your immune system gets a boost and the physical effects of stress gradually drop down.

Massage therapy can also help you to sleep better at night, which leaves you feeling more rested and more able to cope with whatever the day throws at you without resorting to angry outbursts. Regular massage therapy is a good idea for anyone who struggles with anger and is prone to emotional outbursts.

Using Hypnotherapy

Hypnotherapy is a very different way of dealing with anger. Most of the anger management techniques focus on teaching you how to control and manage your anger whereas hypnotherapy goes to the root of the problem – what caused the anger in the first place.

It teaches you how to resolve that anger and remove it from your life so that you can concentrate on and deal with situations more effectively. A hypnotherapist will delve deep into your conscious mind, going beyond that and into your unconscious mind to find the root of the problem.

Hypnotherapy can be used to teach you to change the way you think about things and how you behave by teaching you how to deal with the problem that caused the anger in a more rational and calm manner. It is often teamed with deep breathing and relaxation techniques that you can do anywhere and at any time to help you control your emotions.

In short, it teaches you to be aware of what causes the anger rather than focusing on the anger itself and it helps you learn how to be more flexible and rational in your day-to-day life.

Chapter 11: Aromatherapy

Aromatherapy is actually a very good holistic method of relieving stress and learning to manage your anger. It makes use of essential oils, which are extracted from plants by cold pressing, steam distillation, or a method called absolute, used for oils that would not survive either of the other two methods. Cold pressing is generally used to extract citrus oils and steam is for all other plants.

As well as being a great stress reliever, aromatherapy is also believed to be able to boost the immune system, something that suffers when you are constantly angry, depressed and worn out. The immune system is responsible for fighting off ills and diseases and, when it's down, its out – aromatherapy helps by stimulating certain chemicals in your brain and boosting them to up the ante on your immune system.

One of the most popular ways that aromatherapy is used in anger management is the use of essential oils in massage. The combination of the aroma of the oils, the deep tissue massage and the oils being absorbed through your skin helps to relax you and melt away tension in the muscles and in the mind.

To understand how aromatherapy works, we must understand how the use of scent works on our bodies. When we breathe in air that is infused with the scent of essential oils, it goes straight to the roof of the nose. The olfactory sensors located there then take that information straight to the limbic system, which is where the emotions we feel are processed. Aromatherapy is ideal for treating stress and anger because it helps to stimulate certain brain chemicals that aid relaxation.

A quick word of caution – if you opt to use aromatherapy on your won, rather than going to a trained therapist, you must be aware that some of the essential oils can cause allergies and can also be dangerous if not used correctly. Always test the oil on a small patch of skin before starting and never use more than the instructions say.

Chapter 12: Using Herbal Remedies and Vitamins

Herbs and vitamins are an excellent way of relieving stress and, indeed, they have many benefits over prescribed drugs. For a start, they work more slowly and subtly than prescription strength medications. They are generally not addictive and have few, if any, side effects or drawbacks, provided they are used correctly.

It is always better to try the natural route before heading straight for the doctor and his prescription pad. Natural remedies are easier to obtain and you can moderate how you take them. In addition, even though they may not have much of a physical effect on you, they can help you psychologically and physiologically.

Herbal supplements and vitamins do not have the effect of making you feel drowsy or wiped out. They also don't have the strength that prescription drugs have and do not affect your reactions or way of thinking. Some of the better vitamins and minerals for stress, anxiety and anger are:

B Vitamins

B vitamins are essential to the function of our nerves, in particular, B1, B2 and B6. These three help to remove the lactic acid, which is a contributory factor to panic attacks. Unfortunately, the average diet is severely lacking in these vitamins as many of the processes involved in food making remove them, i.e. milling flour for white bread eliminates many of the essential vitamins.

B vitamins help to regulate mood and assist the amino acids in our bodies to function as they should. These vitamins are not stored in our bodies so they must be taken either through vitamin supplements or through food. They work best taken as a complex with other B vitamins and a lack of them can lead to cravings for sugar, mood changes and problems sleeping.

Magnesium

This mineral is absolutely vital to the function of our bodies as it helps to keep the heartbeat steady, gives our bones strength and helps to keep blood pressure at a normal rate. It is also a necessary mineral in reducing the effects of constant anger, stress and anxiety.

It is used as a muscle relaxant and much research has been done to show the benefits it has in reducing fear, anxiety, anger, nervousness and irritability. It is, in actual fact, probably the most common element found on earth. Sadly, like the B vitamins, the way we produce food these days wipes a lot of it out, leading to depletion in many people.

Real deficiency is not a common thing but it can be reduced enough to have the effect of increasing panic and anxiety, leading to more angry outbursts. That said, certain conditions themselves will decrease magnesium levels in the body, including:

- Stress
- Hyperventilation
- Even some foods can do it.

Magnesium is required for over 300 different metabolic reactions in the human body and is vital for the health of our nerves. That said, taking a magnesium supplement is not going to cure you but it may help to reduce feelings of anxiety. One of the best ways to inject a dose of magnesium into your body is through bathing in water with Epsom salts dissolved in it. The magnesium present in the salts are absorbed through the skin and, combined with a drop of lavender oil, is a fantastic way to feel calm and relaxed while taking in a vital mineral.

 Magnesium is also present in dark leafy greens like cabbage, spinach, kale, beet greens, etc. and these contain B vitamins as well. Eating a diet rich in these, fish, beef, chicken seeds and some fruit swill also boost your magnesium levels.

Inositol

Inositol is a natural carbohydrate that can help to boost neurotransmitter levels in the body, something that is severely affected by anger, stress and anxiety. It is found in low doses in foods such as beans, rice, fruit, and some grains. It helps the brains to produce serotonin, that well-known "feel-good" chemical that makes stress go away and fights against the effects of anxiety.

GABA

GABA stands for Gamma Amino Butyric Acid and, although it sounds like the contents of a prescribed drug, it is actually found naturally in many food sources. It is an amino acid that helps to protect the nerve cells from burning out as a result of excessive and constant angry outbursts and panic attacks. GABA is found in glutamate, which is present in the following foods in differing levels:

- Cow milk
- Eggs
- Mackerel
- Beef
- Chicken
- Corn
- Oysters
- Potatoes
- Tomatoes
- Mushrooms
- Peas
- Broccoli
- Grape Juice
- Soy sauce
- Walnuts
- Parmesan cheese

Herbal Teas

Tea and coffee contains caffeine but herbal and fruit teas don't. Peppermint and chamomile teas promote relaxation and green tea has an amino acid in it that can boost your GABA levels.

Omega Fatty Acids

Omega 3 and 6 essential fatty acids are needed to maintain a good level of both physical and mental health. A balance of them in your body can help to lower the effects the fight or flight response has on the body. While you can take these in capsule form, you can also get them from the foods you eat, especially oily fish.

Kava

This herb has been used for thousands of years to promote relaxations and a sense of wellbeing. It is usually made into a drink that has slight sedative effects and is a good choice for keeping your anger levels under control. It is most commonly sold in tablet form or as a tea and produces a feeling of mild sedation, is a muscle relaxant and is anxiolytic, i.e. it reduces the effects of anxiety.

Other Natural Anti-Anxiety Supplements

There are a wide number of these supplements available but the most common and those that have been shown to have the most effect include:

- Valerian
- Passion flower
- St John's Wort
- Catnip
- Fennel
- Chamomile
- Motherwort
- Skullcap

Vitamin D

Known as the sunlight vitamin, this is generally found in fatty fish like salmon or mackerel and, given exposure to sufficient sunlight, the body can produce its own. Many people find that they are more anxious and prone to outbursts of anger in the winter months and this is when extra vitamin D may be needed.

The fact that vitamin and herbal supplements are abundantly available to purchase does not meant that you can eat what you like and get your requirements from the pills. The best way to manage anger, anxiety, depression and panic is to eat a sensible healthy diet that contains your entire vitamin and mineral needs. It is OK to take supplements to boost your levels though, especially when you are under a great deal of stress.

Top Herbal Remedies for Managing Anger

Lavender

Lavender has long been associated with calming and, used at night it can help to make sure you get a decent night's sleep. Good sleep helps to freshen your mind and keep it relaxed, which helps to control anxiety. Apply a couple of drops of lavender oil to your head and massage it in thoroughly before you go to sleep at night. This will control anger in your mind and send you to a relaxed sleep. If you bathe in the morning, add a few drops of lavender oil to your bath to keep you calm and relaxed throughout the day.

Verbena

Also known as vervain, verbena has long been used to regulate moods and cut down on anger. It contains flavonoids, erodedmonoterpenes and caffeic acid derivatives, which have been shown to help relax neck muscles and shoulder muscles. It provides a calming effect to the brain, thus increasing resistance to anger and can easily be consumed in a tincture.

German Chamomile

German chamomile is one of the most effective herbs for controlling anger and is best consumed as an herbal tea. Chamomile tea is calming and helps to soothe feelings of anger because it contains coumarin, cyanogenic glucoside and choline. These have been proven to be effective at reducing anxiety levels and anger. Chamomile can also be taken in capsule form or as an extract.

Dandelion

Many people think of dandelion as a weed but it is an herb that is very effective at dealing with stress and anger. Dandelion provides a lot of support to the liver, cooling it down and regulating anxiety and anger, as well as keeping you healthy. It can be consumed as a tea, in capsule form or as a tincture but the best result are gained from the capsules.

Skullcap

Skullcap tea is one of the best herbal teas for controlling feelings of anger. The tea can be made from the leaves and the flowers and is a strong remedy for controlling anger, because it contains volatile oils and tannins. Together, these help to reduce hysteria and tension, which also helps with anger control, soothes feelings of anger and calms the brain.

Burdock Root

Burdock root is another herb that helps to counteract angry and anxious feelings in humans. It works best on the liver but can also help with overall healing. The best way to take burdock root is in the form of a tea, consumed on a daily basis. It works to control anger by stabilizing some of the major causes of anger, emotional disturbances in the brain.

St John's Wort

Depression is one of the biggest causes of anger and this herb can help to control the anger caused by depression. This is because it contains volatile oils and xanthones, which are used to help treat depression in humans. Made into a tea and consumed daily, St John's Wort can help to control anger and relive tension.

Oat Seeds

A tincture of oat seeds has long been used as a way of treating anger. Oat seeds contain steroid saponins, silicic acids and polysaccharides, which help to lower cholesterol – high cholesterol levels have been linked with irritation and anger. Oat seeds made into a tincture can help to relieve mild anxiety, balance out the nervous system and control anger.

Using EFT

EFT, or Emotional Freedom Technique is gaining recognition as a form of holistic therapy for anger management. It is used as a way to remove emotional charge, to diffuse situations on a day to day basis and to change the way you think. In fact, it is now probably the top therapy for anger management as it helps you to understand why you are angry, what caused it and why you cannot control it. You will also learn why, however much you try, you cannot control your anger alone and will need some help.

EFT helps with the physical and the emotional side of anger. It is called Acupuncture for the Emotions and the techniques used can have a very powerful effect on the way you handle stress and anger and how you react in certain situations.

The Emotional Freedom Technique is a Tapping Technique that helps you to overcome behaviors that you previously learned. In effect, it is a way of reprogramming your mind, rewiring it, if you like, to react differently and to choose how you react rather than falling back on something you learned earlier in life.

It is one of the most effective methods of anger management and, once you have attended a couple of sessions with a therapist, you will be able to do it yourself, and it can even be carried out over the telephone.

Chapter 13: Top Strategies for Dealing With Anger

We all get angry at times but some people exhibit a kind of rage that is out of control and, in many cases, out of proportion. This isn't healthy, for either the person concerned or the people around them. If you can't control your anger, you have the potential to get involved in violent acts, reckless driving, putting yourself and others in danger. Anger also makes you ill and has been shown to increase the risks of heart disease and strokes. It can also lead to insomnia, headaches and problems with the digestive system.

You can lean to take control of your anger though. One recent study showed that CBT – cognitive behavioral therapy – improved the control over anger and cut down on the amount of hostility and aggression the people studied were exhibiting. Below we look at a few strategies that you can use to take control of your anger and rein it in.

Relaxation

There are a few simple tools that you can use to help you relax, the most popular being deep breathing and visual imagery. Try these steps to help you soothe feelings of anger:

- **Deep Breathing** – Breathe deep from your diaphragm. Breathing from your chest won't do anything so imagine that your breath is coming all the way up from your gut.
- **Repeat a calming phrase or word** - keep on repeating it to yourself while you are breathing deeply. Choose words like "relax" or phrases like "take it easy".
- **Use Imagery** – Either recall a relaxing scene from your past or imagine one and keep it in your mind
- **Slow and Non-Strenuous Exercise** – try Yoga or something similar to relax your muscles and calm you

Practice these on a daily basis and soon you will find that you are doing them automatically when you find yourself in a situation that has the potential to tense you and cause anger.

Cognitive Restructuring

In simple terms, cognitive restructuring means that you change the way that you think. When you are stressed out and angry, your thinking tends to be somewhat dramatic. How many times has something gone awry, you've gotten angry and told yourself that everything is ruined now? When you learn cognitive restructuring, you learn how to replace negative thoughts with reasonable and positive ones. Try these:

- **Never Say Never** - or the word "always" when you are talking about other people or yourself. Using statements like "you're ALWAYS forgetting things" or "this NEVER works" are simply justifying your angry feelings and you are telling yourself that there isn't a way to solve the problem. Remove those words from your vocabulary unless they are absolutely needed and you can't get around using them.

- **Focus on your Goals** – Let's say your friend is always late when you have an arrangement to meet. Instead of getting irritated and going on the attack, turn your focus to what you want to accomplish, your goal. State the issue calmly and then look for a solution that will suit both of you. If that doesn't work, solve it yourself – perhaps tell your friend to meet you a half hour earlier that you actually are going to meet – if he or she is always later, there is a good chance that they will be on time. The problem is solved with no need for angry outbursts.
- **Use Logic** – there are times when anger is wholly justified but it can get out of hand and become irrational. Keep telling yourself that the world is not after you; you are just going through one of the rough spots that are inevitable in life. Do this every time you start feeling angry and you will soon find that your perspective is more balanced.
- **Turn expectations into Desires** – People who are angry are also demanding, whether it is for appreciation, fairness, and agreement or just for people to be willing to do things the way they want them done. We can't always get things our own way and it can be frustrating. It is, however, important that you do not allow that frustration to turn into anger. Make yourself aware that you are demanding and teach yourself to turn those demands into requests instead.

Problem Solving

Anger and frustration can be the result of some very real issues in our lives, issues that we cannot escape from. Anger can be a very healthy response, a natural one to some problems. There are those who believe that every problem has a solution and that belief can increase their frustration when it comes to light that this is not always the case. If you cannot find a solution to the issue or problem that is troubling you, instead, focus on how to face the problem and how to handle it. Make a plan on how to do this and keep a check on how you are progressing along the way. Use an organization or time management guide if need be. Give it your best shot but, if you can't find the answer or solve the issues straightaway, do not give in to frustration and anger.

Better Communication

It is very easy to jump to conclusions when you are angry, no matter how farfetched those conclusions may be. If you are involved in a heated discussion, slow down and listen to what it is being said. Take a time out before your answer; think things through very carefully before you speak. Look at what could be behind your angry feelings. Try not to go on the defensive when you come under criticism, instead try to hear what could be behind what is being said. Be patient, take your time and don't ever let things spin out of control.

Humor

Humor can be helpful in several ways when it comes to defusing an angry rage. It can help you to see things in a better perspective. Let's say you are angry with a colleague for some reason, perhaps because they are constantly slacking off and leaving you to pick up the work. Don't get angry; instead, picture your colleague as something humorous. If you can't picture it in your mind's eye, draw a picture. Either way, you can take the edge off your anger and lessen the tension. Humor is also good when you find yourself being somewhat unreasonable about something. Let's say you think that everything should go your way and, when it doesn't, you find it intolerable. Picture yourself as some kind of god or goddess, one who is forever being deferred to. Add more detail in, and you will soon become aware of just how unreasonable you are being and that what you are angry about really isn't all that important.

I must urge caution with humor though. First, you must never just laugh off your problems Instead use it to face them and deal with them more constructively. Second, don't resort to using sarcastic humor, as this is just another way of being aggressive and angry.

Environmental Change

On occasion, it will be your surroundings that cause the feelings of anger. Responsibilities and problems tend to weigh heavy and make you feel as though you are trapped, resulting in feelings of anger. Look at road rage as an example. If you always get angry when you are driving, you are putting yourself and other road users at risk. Drivers who are angry are aggressive; they take risks and chances and will report more near misses or actual accidents than a more relaxed driver will. If this is you, find either an alternative route or an alternative mode of transport. Try these tips to help you ease up:

- **Have a Break** - make sure you have time for you scheduled into your day, especially in particularly stressful parts of the day. Perhaps make it a rule that, for 15 minutes when you get home, you will have a period of quiet time.
- **Think about the Timing** - if you tend to be more argumentative at night, it is probably because you are tired, distracted or have gotten into the bad habit of fighting then. Change the time when you discuss important things to a time when you are more alert and relaxed.
- **Avoid Things That You can** - If you get angry when you walk past your daughter's tip of a room, close the door. You don't have to look at it if it makes you angry. Don't keep telling yourself that your child has to clean their room because that will just make you angrier. The whole point is to keep calm and not allow anger to creep in.

How a Psychologist Can Help

If you find that you are still overwhelmed with angry feelings and just can't get them under control, you may need to consider seeing a psychologist or another mental health professional. They can help you to pinpoint what is causing the problem and help you learn how to deal with it. Most psychologists use therapy as a form of treatment to help you learn how to make changes for the good and deal with the bad.

Chapter 14: Harnessing the Power of Anger – Women and Anger

No doubt, you know someone who seems to be constantly angry, perhaps even you! The manner in which you cope with those feelings of anger in an important factor in determining your health in the long term. Suppressed anger is responsible for more deaths, more risk of cancer, heart disease and high blood pressure, to name just a few.

Anger is a natural emotion although it tends to be frowned on in women. Many women were never taught to express anger in a positive way, instead being told that it should be avoided at all costs. As such, in adulthood we find it very difficult to untangle and separate feelings of anger from depression and anxiety. The younger generation today will find it easier to cope because they have been brought up in a more liberal way but will still find themselves simmering with anger at times, anger which will explode when least expected.

Anger is a very powerful emotion but used in the right way, it can help to clarify our objectives and guide s through a situation in safety. Used in the wrong way, anger is dangerous. It affects our health and it can have a negative effect on those around us. Thus, we must learn to use anger for the benefits it can give us and understand what causes it, emotionally and biologically.

Fight or Flight

When our bodies sense that we are in danger, it goes into "fight or flight" mode. Fear makes us want to run in the opposite direction, to take flight, away from a potential confrontation. Anger makes us get ready for a fight. These are primal emotions and are designed to help guarantee survival.

In the brain, there are two structures, both almond in shape, that are called amygdala. These are what recognizes danger and sends an alarm bell ringing throughout your system. Your central nervous system goes into overdrive and floods your body with hormones to help the fight. Sometimes, this will happen before your prefrontal cortex, the part of your brain responsible for thinking, is even aware that there is any danger.

Anger causes neurotransmitters in the brain to release energy into your system that lasts for about 5 or 10 minutes. This is adrenaline and it makes your heart beat faster, causes your blood pressure to rise and sends extra blood into your legs and arms. As well as adrenaline, your body is releasing cortisol and norepinephrine, forcing your body into a state of alertness, ready for the fight. You may even stop thinking and this is why you find that you have said or done things that you don't really remember.

This works exactly the same in every single person. The differences lie in how you control that instinct and that control relies on a number of different factors – physiological, emotional, biological, learned and gender related.

Women and Anger

Society seems to be more accepting of anger in men, that men are more aggressive and protective. To a large extent, angry outbursts in men are ignored while the same in a woman is strongly frowned upon. In biological terms, both high and low levels of the male hormone, testosterone, have been linked to aggression in men. Women may also suffer with aggression and irritability if they have an imbalance of testosterone but it is expressed in a different way. What is not clear at this stage is whether people who are angry generate more testosterone or if high levels of the hormone cause the anger.

Men are more likely to respond in anger to another person or object, thus externalizing their feelings, while women internalize, or direct that anger inwards or towards others in a more indirect manner. Younger women have learned to cope better and to express their anger in a healthier manner but the anger is often misdirected towards a target that is seen as safe, such as their children or spouse, instead of towards the primary source. Everyone, no matter what gender or age, has to learn how to deal with anger in an appropriate way.

Think about this. The health risks that are associated with hostility and anger in men are just as likely to be true of women. Think about what your anger is costing you in terms of health, family, career and your personal life. On the other hand, it is not healthy to stifle your anger. It doesn't make the angry feelings disappear, it just makes them worse. In fact, showing your anger in a hostile way and stifling it works exactly the same. Stifling it now is more likely to see it come out in anther hostile way at another time, or as anxiety, depression, resentment, pain, self-destructive behavior, irritability or addictive behavior.

In order to know when your anger is being deal with in a healthy and positive manner, you first have to understand what activates that anger. If you can pinpoint the trigger and work out how you should control the anger, you can express it in a more appropriate way and at a more appropriate time. Instead of being negative and out of control, your anger will be more constructive and you will not feel guilty or shameful about your outburst.

Common Roots of Anger in Women

Anger is an emotion that is primitive in nature and may even be because of something experienced while you were still in the womb. Anger triggers are learned behaviors – for example, if you were raised by a parent who was angry or in a household that was explosive (alcoholic, drug dependent, etc.), there is a very good chance that your brain has learned these behaviors are normal.

Let's take it a step further and assume that one or both of your parents were passive-aggressive, controlling or suppressing their anger; this is also a part of your internal experience. If you witnessed or were a victim of abuse, you may suppress anger, perhaps without knowing it, and this may surface many years down the road. Children model their behavior on the adults around them and they will pass the behavior on unless they make a conscious decision that they will change the cycle they are caught in and put a stop to it.

Have you ever heard of "good girl syndrome"? Perhaps you were a peacekeeper between argumentative parents. You had a passive submissive parent and an aggressive dominant parent and you tried to be the good girl, keeping the peace between them two, to try to make things better. That can create suppressed anger that may surface at any time, without warning.

There are other anger triggers as well, not least your diet. Another term that you may hear on occasion is "hangry". This is something you feel when your body is not receiving the right nutrition throughout the course of the day and your mood moves into Hungry-Angry mode. To get round this, make sure you eat three balanced meals per day and two balanced snacks to keep your moods on an even keel. If you skip a meal and then find yourself totally overreacting to minor issues, you will know that it is hunger that is affecting your emotions and causing your anger response. It may just be mild irritation but this may also be the beginning of something more volatile so make sure you are eating regularly throughout the day.

It isn't just when you eat; it is also what you eat that counts. If you exist on what seems to be the standard diet of high fat, high sugar and processed foods, you are going to be irritable. If you eat a diet that is lower in damaged saturated fats, (the kind you find in processed and fast foods), you will experience less feelings of hostility, depression and your cholesterol levels will be lower too.

A balanced meal should contain the right mix of lean protein, healthy fat and plenty of fresh vegetables that are not loaded with starch. It should have a low GI loading, thus allowing your blood sugar levels to even out which will keep your temper in check. A diet such as this will keep the levels of serotonin and cortisol in your body on an even keel, thus calming your mind and brain. It isn't just children that are liable to temper tantrums; adults that live on a diet of high GI foods are also liable to lose their temper, especially if they are already suffering with stress of some description. Another rule to live by – the contents of your plate should be colorful – high colored fruits and vegetables contain higher levels of antioxidants, vitamins and nutrients, thus ensuring you get all you need on a daily basis.

Eating a diet filed with unhealthy sugars and fats will stress your liver with an overload of toxins that it can't cope with. Your liver must be in tiptop condition if you want to digest these kinds of foods properly, because it has to create more bile. The precise meaning of "bilious" is irritable so the more bile your liver has to create, the more your moods will deteriorate.

If your serotonin levels are low, this can cause anger related to poor nutrition. Depression is, in real terms, anger that has been turned upon yourself. Taking antidepressants may make you feel better for a while because it boosts your serotonin levels. However, while your anger is being treated as depression, the real cause remains unknown and, in the long-term, the treatment will not work. Both depression and anger are strongly influenced by a hormonal imbalance and this is why women who are menopausal or perimenopasual may show symptoms of both.

What is the Connection between Hormones and Anger?

Irritability and mood swings are two of the symptoms caused by fluctuations in hormone levels. They are generally experienced more during pregnancy, the menstrual cycle, perimenopause and the menopause. Angry emotions create pro-inflammatory molecules in your body – estrogen has a somewhat anti-inflammatory quality while progesterone is calming. This explains why some women are angrier when their hormone levels become erratic and some will experience either a testosterone imbalance or a dominance of cortisol, leading to anxiety and anger. Many women who enter perimenopause or the menopause are surprised at the anger they feel, not realizing that the hormonal imbalance is similar to that experienced in the menstrual cycle. The menopause is also a time when real feelings of anger are expressed, more so than at any other time.

Try seeing your anger as a power source. Anger is a strong emotion that you can use to help you fight for what's yours. This is a time to stand up for your own beliefs, for yourself but only if you learn to channel that anger and use it in a positive manner.

Nobody wants to be associated with a person who is angry or irritable. To express your anger properly, your brain has to learn to think before you act, especially in the case of a person who is impulsive and lashes out for no apparent reason. You must be certain that there isn't a physical reason for your anger. Speak with your doctor and get yourself checked out It isn't all that common but a brain tumor can cause pressure to build up and that can provoke an aggressive response.

The following are a few things you can take into consideration to ensure you are living a healthy lifestyle:

Support your serotonin and hormonal levels with the right nutrition – Take a multivitamin or mineral complex every day but make sure that it is pharmaceutical grade to get the best out of it. It must be rich in magnesium and calcium and you should also add in a high quality omega-3 fatty acid supplement as well. Don't eat foods that contain damaged fats, processed foods, or simple sugars Instead, eat healthy fats, like extra virgin olive oil, foods that contain high levels of omega-3. If your anger is related to PMS or the perimenopause, you might need to take a progesterone supplement to restore the ratios in your body.

Support your live - A healthy diet will do wonders for your liver but you can give it a helping hand and a clean slate to work from by doing a detoxification program. Cut the alcohol as it contributes towards anger, hostility and depression. Take supplements that help to cleanse the liver or use herbs like dandelion and milk thistle. Drink at least 2 liters of water daily, as this will help to keep your liver flushed out.

Support your nervous system – Cut out or cut back on nicotine and caffeine intake. These are both harsh on the central nervous system. Make sure you take omega-3 supplements, especially EPA and DHA, as these work to insulate your nerve cells and protect them.

Track your anger patterns in a diary – Write down when you become irritable and angry. Perhaps it is certain times of the month or after you have eaten specific foods, or a specific circumstance that triggers it. If you can learn the pattern, learn the triggers, your can teach your body and brain to react in a more positive way, allowing the thinking part of the brain to take over control. Trust me when I say that counting to ten does work because it gives your brain a chance to catch up and take over.

Learn how to cope in the moment – As well as counting to ten, or twenty if needs be, teach yourself how to breathe deeply. Learn meditation techniques, visualization or just walk away from the source of that anger. Once the angry feelings have gone, take the time out to study your emotions and find a more productive way to release that anger.

Use physical activity to release the anger - go to the gym or go for a run. Turn up your music and dance. Learn primal screaming techniques, pound out your anger on a pillow or a punch bag or go and dig the garden. Just find some productive physical and safe way to work the anger out of your system.

Use creativity to channel your anger - sometimes, getting creative can be a healthy and safe outlet for your anger. Prepare a nice meal, pain the house, start a craft project, take up singing or dancing. It doesn't matter what it is as long as your creative side can come out and your anger can be channeled positively.

Give your anger a voice – but not while you are still angry. Once you have removed the feelings of anger and you have calmed down, speak about it. Don't ever direct your anger at a person but do talk about why it hurts and how it makes you feel. If you can't talk about it, write it down. Some people food that writing it all down and then burning it can help to decrease the feelings of anger, helping them to react more rationally, in a way that does not eave feelings of guilt and shame.

Don't be afraid to ask for help or support – Anger is a very complex emotion and there is a chance that it has been building up inside of you for a long time. If you can't explore your own feelings, can't identify the pattern of your anger, consider asking for support in the form of emotional freedom techniques or talk with a therapist. The real key is to know where your feelings come from and you have to know this before you can develop the skills to help you cope with them.

In all truthfulness, angry women can actually be a good source for changing things for the better. Injustice and intolerance can be effectively fought using feelings of anger and the responses to those feelings. However, those feelings must be used in the right way because misplaced anger or continuing anger takes away the power to effect change and it can also take a terrible toll on your health. Start thinking about how you can put your anger in a place that will help you rather than in a pale where you keep tripping over it. Start to understand where your anger comes from, how to use and what it can do. Start to learn how to turn negativity into positivity and make your world a better and healthier place to be.

Conclusion

The holistic approach to anger management is gaining ground every day as more and more people turn away from pills and potions and turn towards a more natural way of healing.

More treatments take the holistic approach as it focuses on the whole of the person, not just one small part. Holistic therapy treats what is seen as an imbalance rather than a specific pain or symptom, thus healing the whole body. Panic attacks, anxiety and anger are all seen as an imbalance of behavior, emotions, thoughts and the nerves and, as such, treatments such as yoga, acupuncture, reiki and massage are employed to help treat the cause rather than the effect.

Methods such as meditation and deep breathing are many thousands of years old. They are natural and they promote a natural and healthy lifestyle. The holistic approach to anger management will introduce you to herbs, vitamins and minerals; it will teach you the role they play in your well-being and how to get them through diet. It will also help you to understand your body and your mind as well as your soul.

While you can undertake any of these methods on your own, if you suffer with serious anger management issues you should see a doctor and draw up a proper plan of treatment, involving these methods, with the proper specialists on hand to ensure you follow the plan effectively.

You May Enjoy James Seal's Other Books

Personality Disorders: Borderline Personality Disorder: Beauty Queen or Emotional Terrorist?

hyperurl.co/emotionalterror

NLP Subconscious Mind Power: Change Your Mind Change Your Life

hyperurl.co/NLP

Creativity : Creative Thinking To Improve Memory, Increase Success and Live A Healthy Life hyperurl.co/creative

SELF ESTEEM: Confidence Building: Overcome Fear, Stress and Anxiety: Self Help Guide

hyperurl.co/selfesteem

Personality Disorders: NARCISSISM: How To Survive A Narcissistic Relationship

hyperurl.co/narcissism

Psychopath: Inside The Mind Of Predators and Con Men: Personality Disorders

hyperurl.co/psychopath

Printed in Great Britain
by Amazon.co.uk, Ltd.,
Marston Gate.